How to Find Unclaimed Money in Virginia and West Virginia

I0450190

Gary L. Morris

Table of Contents

Virginia

West Virginia

Introduction

In Virginia the Unclaimed Property Department collects and oversees money and other properties which have been unclaimed by Virginia residents for a period of three to five years. Rightful owners or their heirs always have the right to claim funds held by the State in the Unclaimed Property Fund; there is no time limit for you to claim this money.

Millions of dollars in unclaimed assets in Virginia are ready to be claimed, and much of this money belongs to people who don't even know the funds exist. If you or any of your relatives of past generations has lived in Virginia, it's possible some of that money could be yours.

The State of Virginia, like many states does not have the resources to investigate every individual case, and are able to do little more than advertise the names of owners in local newspapers. The resulting void is filled by professional "finders" who locate the owners and charge a fee or commission in exchange for returning it. Sometimes those fees are outrageous, but people are willing to pay them, as the finder has uncovered funds they would not otherwise have, or even know about.

The truth is that with the right information, you can claim that money yourself and avoid falling victim to scammers or having to pay those high commissions. This guide to claiming unclaimed funds in Virginia contains all the information you need laid out in an easy to follow step-by-step manner. We'll show you what to do, how to do it, and when and where to file your claim.

How to Identify Unclaimed Money in Virginia

There are many types of personal property that fall under Virginia Unclaimed Property Laws, but generally they fall into three different categories; securities related property, investment, trading and broker/dealer and fiduciary property, and general ledger property. The State of Virginia may also hold unclaimed property for profit and non-profit organizations such as financial institutions, retail stores, local governments, churches, communities, restaurants, clubs, and associations etc.

Under the three major categories come multiple sub-groups as follows:

Securities-Related Property

Cash or Stock Dividends
Bond Interest
PIK Payments
Redemption Values
Warrants
Cash Dividend (ADR), Stock Dividends (ADR)
Other Distributions Resulting from Ownership of Interest or Dept. Obligation
Un-exchanged Shares
Cash in Lieu
Bond Principal: Matured and Called
Mutual Fund Shares: Book, Dividend Reinvestment or Cash

Investment, Trading and Broker/Dealer and Fiduciary Property

Cash Over Receipts (Dividends and Other)
Bond Interest Over Receipts
Stock Over Receipts (Dividends and Other Memos)
Other Distributions Resulting from Ownership of Interest or Debt Obligation
Fiduciary Checks
Distribution, Expenses, etc.
Surplus from Sale of Pledged Property
Securities in Customers' Trading, Investment Trust Accounts

Securities Held in a Vault or Storage Area of a Bank
Securities Found in a Safe Deposit Box
Credit Balances in Trading and Trusts, Brokers, Investment Firms, or Cash etc.

General Ledger Property

Negotiable Instruments

Certified Checks, Cashier Checks, Registered Checks
Bank Money Orders
Drafts, Warrants
Travellers Checks, Personal Money Orders

Account Balances

Demand Deposits
Saving Accounts, Club Accounts
Security Deposits
Retirement Accounts
Matured Certificates of Deposits
 Collateral Deposits, Unidentified Deposits
 Remittances and Suspense Accounts
 Credit Balances Arising from Loans (Includes Liquidated Mortgages)
 Remainder of Collateral Amounts Credit Balance
 Consumer Credit Accounts
 Credit Balances or Cash Due Renters

Insurance Proceeds and Property

Limited Age (Superannuated) Contracts
Matured Endowments
Death Claims
Amounts Due under Policy of Non-Life Insurance
Refunds and Other Amounts Due Under Policy Terms Companies
Accident and Health Payments, Annuity Payments
Agent's Credit Balance
Policy Dividends
Claims Payments for Liquidated Obligations

Experience Rating Refunds
Worker Compensation Benefits
Stock Over Receipts
Any Other Amounts Due Under Policy Terms

General Ledger Items

Wages, Payroll Salaries, Commissions
Outstanding Checks Issued to Vendors
Expense Checks
Amounts Owed by Sales and Insurance Finance Companies
Pension Checks
Credit Checks or Memos
Mineral Proceeds
Royalties
Utility Service
Advance Payments for Utility Service Not-Furnished
Refunds Due from Insurance Companies

The above listing is not exhaustive, but it covers the vast majority of what is can be claimed as unclaimed property in Virginia.

What Does Not Qualify as Unclaimed Money in Virginia

Unclaimed property does not include overpaid contributions by employers to the unemployment compensation fund, real estate, vehicles or most tangible property

Gift certificates, gift cards, or in-store merchandise credit issued or maintained by any person engaged primarily in the business of selling tangible personal property at retail

Property held, due, and owing in a foreign country and arising out of a foreign transaction

Abandoned vehicles, real estate, furniture and stolen property

How to Claim Your Property or Funds in Virginia

By law, all businesses must check their records on an annual basis to determine if they are in possession of unclaimed funds. If so, they are to file a report with the Unclaimed Property Department and turn over their holdings to the Virginia Unclaimed Property Fund.

Any individual claiming an interest in any property or funds handed over to the state is entitled to file a claim on forms furnished by the Unclaimed Property Department. There are several steps you must take to claim unclaimed property in Virginia.

The first option is to search for your name in the **Virginia Unclaimed Property Fund Database**. If you find your name and associated property you will be given the option to submit a Claim online. Once you confirm that you are the owner of the property you will be given the option to receive a check by mail or have the funds deposited directly to an account in your name.

Virginia Unclaimed Property Fund Database:
https://www.trs.virginia.gov/vaMoneySearch/Account/LogOn

Owners of unclaimed property in the Virginia Unclaimed Property Fund must provide proof of identification with their returned claim form and claimant's signature must be notarized. The documentation additionally required is generally as follows:

Individual Owner

All US citizens must provide a copy of their Social Security or Medicare Card. Additionally you may be required to provide one or more of the following:

Driver's License
Birth Certificate
Passport
Non-Driver Identification Card
Marriage Certificate
Social Insurance Card
Social Security Card

W-2
National Identity Card
Medicare Card
Election Card
Citizenship Card

If there is a **Joint Owner** they must provide the same.

Heir, Trustee, Personal Representative, Executor

If you are inquiring about property not listed in your name you must provide documentation showing you have a legal right to claim the property in addition to the information above. Proof of legal right to claim for another individual includes but is not limited to:

Copies of Appointment to Estate
Letters Testamentary
Small Estate Affidavit
Copy of a Notarized Power of Attorney for a Living Person
Verification of Court Appointed Guardianship
Copy of a Minor's Birth Certificate
Please note that a power of attorney and related documents become void after death. Certified copies of wills can be obtained from the county courthouse where the will was filed.

If you require Virginia Birth, Death, Marriage, Civil Union or Divorce Records contact:

Virginia Department of Health
Vital Records Division
P. O. Box 1000
Richmond, Virginia 23218
Tel: 804-662-6200

E-mail: VitalRec.Questions@vdh.virginia.gov

Virginia Department of Health:http://www.vdh.state.va.us/vital_records/

If you require further information you can write to:

Virginia Department of the Treasury
101 North 14th Street
Richmond, VA 23219

Tel:(804) 225-2393
Toll Free:(800) 468-1088

When You Receive Your Claim Form in the Mail

When you receive your claim form in the mail and you are the owner
of the property, you must follow the instructions within, and
then mail them the required documents along with the original form.
Processing may take up to 12 weeks, and Stock claims may take
longer to process.

If you are NOT the owner listed on the front of the card or an heir of
them you CAN NOT use the mail card as your claim form.

If Money Has Not Been Turned Over to the State

There may be money belonging to you or a family member that has not been turned over to the state. That money however does not have the same regulations governing it or protection that money held in trust by the state does. These types of unclaimed funds are known as "Pre-Escheat" and may take some time and effort to find, but it could be worth it in the long run.

You may be contacted by an agency stating that they have found money in your name and for a percentage they can get it for you. Don't immediately respond to this, as there are steps you can take to uncover such funds and secure them on your own.

In most states unclaimed property must be reported and handed over to the state within a three to five year period. For some types of property however, that period can extend to up to fifteen years. Such funds remain in the hands of corporations until the reporting period is due, and as such you will need to search the corporation itself for your money.

Usually unclaimed money held by corporations remains unclaimed due to mergers or name changes. In the case of mergers, stocks may be split between the two companies, and shares are lost in the process. For this reason you must check the initial incorporation of the company and its history thereafter. Massachusetts, New York, Delaware and Illinois are popular states for the incorporation of companies as laws in those states are favourable, so check those states first.

Trust companies and banks known as "transfer agents" are responsible for informing claimants of capitol changes, and they can be contacted directly. If you suspect you may have money due you because of the above scenarios, you can contact the appropriate agent. Listed on the following pages are some of the major transfer agents for the United States and Canada with links to their websites.

USA

American Stock Transfer & Trust
Tel: 1-800-937-5449

Website: http://www.amstock.com

Bank Of New York
Tel: (800) 524-4458

Website: http://stockbny.com

Equiserve
Tel: (800) 543-3038

Website: http://www.equiserve.com

ChaseMellon Services
Tel: 201-296-4463

Website: http://www.chasemellon.com

Fifth Third Bank
Tel: 513-579-4350

Website: http://www.53.com

First Union National Bank
Tel: 1-800-829-8432

Website: http://www.firstunion.com

Oxford Transfer
Tel: 1-503-225-0375

Website: http://www.transfer.com

Registrar and Transfer Company
Tel: 1-800-368-5948

Website: http://www.rtco.com/

StockTrans, Incorporated
Tel: 1-800-733-1121

Website: http://www.stocktrans.com

Sky Financial Group - Sky Bank
TOLL FREE: 1-800-576-5007
Tel: 419-327-6300

Website: http://www.skyfi.com

U.S. Stock Transfer Corporation
Tel: 1-800-835-8778

Website: www.usstock.com

Wells Fargo-Shareholder Relations
TOLL FREE: 1-800-468-9716
Tel: 651-450-4190

Website: www.wellsfargo.com

Canada

CIBC Mellon
Tel: 1-800-387-0825

Website: http://www.cibcmellon.com

Computershare
Tel:(888) 404-6333

Website: http://www.computershare.com

Federal Resources for Finding Unclaimed Money

There are also other state and nation-wide agencies and organizations that may hold unclaimed property for Virginia residents. Below is a listing of Federal Unclaimed Property Offices that should be checked if you are an Virginia resident searching for unclaimed money or property.

US Department of Housing and Urban Development - If you paid off an FHA mortgage before November 5, 1990, you may be entitled to a refund. In Virginia you can contact:

Richmond Field Office
600 East Broad Street
3rd Floor
Richmond, VA 23219-4920

Tel: (804) 822-4805
Fax:(804) 822-4984
Email: VA_Webmanager@hud.gov

Or you can visit the HUD website where they have a **Get a Refund** search engine.

Get a Refund:
http://www.hud.gov/offices/hsg/comp/refunds/index.cfm

Pension Benefit Guaranty Corporation - Maintains a database of 12,000 individuals who are owed close to $30million in unclaimed pension benefits. Their website features a Find an **Unclaimed Pension Tool** that can be searched by name for unclaimed pension funds. The database information about people whom PBGC has not been able to contact and does not contain information about all individuals for whom PBGC provides, or will in the future provide, a pension.

Unclaimed Pension Tool: http://search.pbgc.gov/mp/mp.aspx

The **Social Security Administration** also maintains records of individuals who qualify for certain pension benefits. When anyone applies for Social Security benefits, their name and Social Security Number are automatically checked against the pension records database and are informed if there are any matches.

Social Security Administration: http://www.ssa.gov/

The Employee Benefits Security Administration (EBSI) – This agency oversees retirement funds, ensuring that retirees receive the monies due to them. Their website features an **Abandoned Plan Search** tool that locates terminated retirement plans or retirement plans that are in the process of being terminated. You will need to know the name of the Retirement plan, and employer, as well as the City and State where the plan was implemented.

Employee Benefits Security Administration:
http://www.dol.gov/ebsa/

Abandoned Plan Search:
http://askebsa.dol.gov/AbandonedPlanSearch/

Federal Deposit Insurance Corporation – When a financial institution is closed by a regulatory agency, the FDIC is appointed as Receiver and is responsible for the payment of insured deposits and the liquidation of the remaining assets.

If you remember a bank account that you had forgotten about you can contact the Federal Deposit Insurance Corporation's (FDIC) Division of Resolutions and Receiverships (DRR) at 1-888-206-4662. They are able to assist consumers in tracking down the current location of accounts and recovering their funds.

You can also search a database of failed banks for accounts, including IRAs using the **FDIC Search Engine**. The search engine is ultra-sensitive to name spellings, so try several variations of your name, for instance; with and without a period after the middle initial, or with and without the middle name or middle initial, etc.

Federal Deposit Insurance Corporation:
http://www2.fdic.gov/funds/index.asp

FDIC Search Engine: http://www2.fdic.gov/funds/index.asp

Internal Revenue Service

If you believe that you are entitled to an unclaimed income tax refund, you should contact the IRS for information on how to obtain it. There are two particular types of unclaimed income tax refund:

Unfiled Income Tax Return. If you did not file a federal income tax return but believe you are due a refund, you must file a return in order to claim it. The average unclaimed refund is around $550. Federal income tax returns must be filed within three years in order for you to receive any refunds you are entitled to.
Filed an Income Tax Return. If you filed a tax return but the check was returned to the IRS as undeliverable (perhaps you relocated and neglected to change your address with the IRS), you should visit their **Where's My Refund** web page to check the status of your refund and where you can also update your details.

Where's My Refund: http://www.irs.gov/Refunds/Where's-My-Refund-It's-Quick,-Easy,-and-Secure.

You can also telephone the IRS at 1-800-829-1954. The average amount of returned refund checks is approximately $1,150.

National Registry of Unclaimed Retirement Benefits (NRURB) - operated by PenChecks, Inc., the NRURB is the largest processor of retirement plan distributions in the United States. The registry is designed to reunite abandoned retirement plans such as pensions, 401(k)s, IRAs, and profit sharing plans with their owners.

Their database contains the names of more than 50,000 individuals who are owed retirement plan distributions, most between $500 and $1,000 in value.

National Registry of Unclaimed Retirement Benefits:
https://www.unclaimedretirementbenefits.com/

Federal Information Center

If you suspect that a Federal agency has money or property belonging to you, but need their contact number, try calling the Federal Information Center at 1-301-722-9000 or the Federal Citizen Information Center at 1-800-FED-INFO (1-800-333-4636). They can direct you to the Federal office you need to contact.

Life Insurance Company Demutualization

Many of the nation's largest life insurance companies were stated as mutual life companies, which are owned by the policyholders. When these companies became publicly traded firms through a process known as demutualization, shares of stock were issued to the policyholders in exchange for their ownership interest. When the address of the policyholder was unknown, the shares and any dividends were put into a trust fund. There are millions of policyholders, as well as their heirs, who could be entitled to these funds.

Glenn Daily, a fee-only insurance consultant, maintains a database depicting the **Reorganization Status of Mutual Life Insurance Companies** on his website. If you find your insurance company in the listing and believe you might be owed shares or money from the proceeds of the demutualization, you should contact the company directly. Be aware that if the demutualization happened more than five years ago, you will most likely be referred to the state unclaimed property office.

Reorganization Status of Mutual Life Insurance Companies:
http://www.glenndaily.com/mhctable.htm

How to Identify Unclaimed Money in West Virginia

There are many types of personal property that fall under West Virginia Unclaimed Property Laws, but generally they fall into three different categories; securities related property, investment, trading and broker/dealer and fiduciary property, and general ledger property. The State of West Virginia may also hold unclaimed property for profit and non-profit organizations such as financial institutions, retail stores, local governments, churches, communities, restaurants, clubs, and associations etc.

Under the three major categories come multiple sub-groups as follows:

Securities-Related Property

Cash or Stock Dividends
Bond Interest
PIK Payments
Redemption Values
Warrants
Cash Dividend (ADR), Stock Dividends (ADR)
Other Distributions Resulting from Ownership of Interest or Dept.
Obligation
Un-exchanged Shares
Cash in Lieu
Bond Principal: Matured and Called
Mutual Fund Shares: Book, Dividend Reinvestment or Cash

Investment, Trading and Broker/Dealer and Fiduciary Property

Cash Over Receipts (Dividends and Other)
Bond Interest Over Receipts
Stock Over Receipts (Dividends and Other Memos)
Other Distributions Resulting from Ownership of Interest or Debt
Obligation
Fiduciary Checks
Distribution, Expenses, etc.
Surplus from Sale of Pledged Property

Securities in Customers' Trading, Investment Trust Accounts
Securities Held in a Vault or Storage Area of a Bank
Securities Found in a Safe Deposit Box
Credit Balances in Trading and Trusts, Brokers, Investment Firms,
or Cash etc.

General Ledger Property

Negotiable Instruments

Certified Checks, Cashier Checks, Registered Checks
Bank Money Orders
Drafts, Warrants
Travellers Checks, Personal Money Orders

Account Balances

Demand Deposits
 Saving Accounts, Club Accounts
 Security Deposits
 Retirement Accounts
 Matured Certificates of Deposits
 Collateral Deposits, Unidentified Deposits
 Remittances and Suspense Accounts
 Credit Balances Arising from Loans (Includes Liquidated
Mortgages)
 Remainder of Collateral Amounts Credit Balance
 Consumer Credit Accounts
 Credit Balances or Cash Due Renters

Insurance Proceeds and Property

Limited Age (Superannuated) Contracts
Matured Endowments
Death Claims
Amounts Due under Policy of Non-Life Insurance
Refunds and Other Amounts Due Under Policy Terms Companies
Accident and Health Payments, Annuity Payments
Agent's Credit Balance

Policy Dividends
Claims Payments for Liquidated Obligations
Experience Rating Refunds
Worker Compensation Benefits
Stock Over Receipts
Any Other Amounts Due Under Policy Terms

General Ledger Items

Wages, Payroll Salaries, Commissions
Outstanding Checks Issued to Vendors
Expense Checks
Amounts Owed by Sales and Insurance Finance Companies
Pension Checks
Credit Checks or Memos
Mineral Proceeds
Royalties
Utility Service
Advance Payments for Utility Service Not-Furnished
Refunds Due from Insurance Companies

The above listing is not exhaustive, but it covers the vast majority of what is can be claimed as unclaimed property in West Virginia.

What Does Not Qualify as Unclaimed Money in West Virginia

Unclaimed property does not include overpaid contributions by employers to the unemployment compensation fund, real estate, vehicles or most tangible property
Gift certificates, gift cards, or in-store merchandise credit issued or maintained by any person engaged primarily in the business of selling tangible personal property at retail
Property held, due, and owing in a foreign country and arising out of a foreign transaction
Abandoned vehicles, real estate, furniture and stolen property

How to Claim Your Property or Funds in West Virginia

By law, all businesses must check their records on an annual basis to determine if they are in possession of unclaimed funds. If so, they are to file a report with the Office of the State Treasurer and turn over their holdings to the West Virginia Unclaimed Property Fund.

Any individual claiming an interest in any property or funds handed over to the state is entitled to file a claim on forms furnished by the Office of the State Treasurer. There are several steps you must take to claim unclaimed property in West Virginia.

The first option is to search for your name in the **West Virginia Unclaimed Property Fund Database**. If you find your name and associated property you will be given the option to submit a Claim online. Once you confirm that you are the owner of the property you will be given the option to receive a check by mail or have the funds deposited directly to an account in your name.

West Virginia Unclaimed Property Fund Database:
http://www.wvsto.com/dept/UP/Pages/default.aspx

Owners of unclaimed property in the West Virginia Unclaimed Property Fund must provide proof of identification with their returned claim form and claimant's signature must be notarized. The documentation additionally required is generally as follows:

Individual Owner

All US citizens must provide a copy of their Social Security or Medicare Card. Additionally you may be required to provide one or more of the following:

Driver's License
Birth Certificate
Passport
Non-Driver Identification Card
Marriage Certificate
Social Insurance Card

Social Security Card
W-2
National Identity Card
Medicare Card
Election Card
Citizenship Card

If there is a **Joint Owner** they must provide the same.

Heir, Trustee, Personal Representative, Executor

If you are inquiring about property not listed in your name you must provide documentation showing you have a legal right to claim the property in addition to the information above. Proof of legal right to claim for another individual includes but is not limited to:

Copies of Appointment to Estate
Letters Testamentary
Small Estate Affidavit
Copy of a Notarized Power of Attorney for a Living Person
Verification of Court Appointed Guardianship
Copy of a Minor's Birth Certificate

Please note that a power of attorney and related documents become void after death. Certified copies of wills can be obtained from the county courthouse where the will was filed.

If you require West Virginia Birth, Death, Marriage, Civil Union or Divorce Records contact:

West Virginia Health Statistics Center
350 Capital St., Room 165
Charleston, WV 25301-3701
Tel: 304-558-2931

West Virginia Health Statistics Center:
http://www.wvdhhr.org/bph/hsc/vital/genealogy.asp

If you require further information you can write to:

West Virginia State Treasurer's Office
Unclaimed Property Division
One Players Club Drive
Charleston, West Virginia 25311

Tel:304-558-2937 Toll Free: 800-642-8687

When You Receive Your Claim Form in the Mail

When you receive your claim form in the mail and you are the owner
of the property, you must follow the instructions within, and
then mail them the required documents along with the original form.
Processing may take up to 12 weeks, and Stock claims may take
longer to process.

If you are NOT the owner listed on the front of the card or an heir of
them you CAN NOT use the mail card as your claim form.

If Money Has Not Been Turned Over to the State

There may be money belonging to you or a family member that has not been turned over to the state. That money however does not have the same regulations governing it or protection that money held in trust by the state does. These types of unclaimed funds are known as "Pre-Escheat" and may take some time and effort to find, but it could be worth it in the long run.

You may be contacted by an agency stating that they have found money in your name and for a percentage they can get it for you. Don't immediately respond to this, as there are steps you can take to uncover such funds and secure them on your own.

In most states unclaimed property must be reported and handed over to the state within a three to five year period. For some types of property however, that period can extend to up to fifteen years. Such funds remain in the hands of corporations until the reporting period is due, and as such you will need to search the corporation itself for your money.

Usually unclaimed money held by corporations remains unclaimed due to mergers or name changes. In the case of mergers, stocks may be split between the two companies, and shares are lost in the process. For this reason you must check the initial incorporation of the company and its history thereafter. Massachusetts, New York, Delaware and Illinois are popular states for the incorporation of companies as laws in those states are favourable, so check those states first.

Trust companies and banks known as "transfer agents" are responsible for informing claimants of capitol changes, and they can be contacted directly. If you suspect you may have money due you because of the above scenarios, you can contact the appropriate agent. Listed on the next pages are some of the major transfer agents for the United States and Canada with links to their websites.

USA

American Stock Transfer & Trust
Tel: 1-800-937-5449

American Stock Transfer & Trust: http://www.amstock.com

Bank Of New York
Tel: (800) 524-4458

Bank Of New York: http://stockbny.com

Equiserve
Tel: (800) 543-3038

Equiserve: http://www.equiserve.com

ChaseMellon Services
Tel: 201-296-4463

ChaseMellon Services: http://www.chasemellon.com

Fifth Third Bank
Tel: 513-579-4350

Fifth Third Bank: http://www.53.com

First Union National Bank
Tel: 1-800-829-8432

First Union National Bank: http://www.firstunion.com

Oxford Transfer
Tel: 1-503-225-0375

Oxford Transfer: http://www.transfer.com

Registrar and Transfer Company
Tel: 1-800-368-5948

Registrar and Transfer Company: http://www.rtco.com/

StockTrans, Incorporated
Tel: 1-800-733-1121

StockTrans, Incorporated: http://www.stocktrans.com

Sky Financial Group - Sky Bank
TOLL FREE: 1-800-576-5007
Tel: 419-327-6300

Sky Financial Group - Sky Bank: http://www.skyfi.com

U.S. Stock Transfer Corporation
Tel: 1-800-835-8778

U.S. Stock Transfer Corporation: www.usstock.com

Wells Fargo-Shareholder Relations
TOLL FREE: 1-800-468-9716
Tel: 651-450-4190

Wells Fargo-Shareholder Relations: www.wellsfargo.com

Canada

CIBC Mellon
Tel: 1-800-387-0825

CIBC Mellon link to: http://www.cibcmellon.com

Computershare: http://www.computershare.com
Tel :(888) 404-6333
Federal Resources for Finding Unclaimed Money

There are also other state and nation-wide agencies and organizations that may hold unclaimed property for West Virginia residents. Below is a listing of Federal Unclaimed Property Offices that should be checked if you are a West Virginia resident searching for unclaimed money or property.

US Department of Housing and Urban Development - If you paid off an FHA mortgage before November 5, 1990, you may be entitled to a refund. In West Virginia you can contact:

Charleston Field Office
405 Capitol Street
Suite 708
Charleston, WV 25301-1795
Tel:(304) 347-7000
Fax: (304) 347-7050

Email: WV_Webmanager@hud.gov

Or you can visit the HUD website where they have a **Get a Refund** search engine.

Get a Refund:
http://www.hud.gov/offices/hsg/comp/refunds/index.cfm

Pension Benefit Guaranty Corporation - Maintains a database of 12,000 individuals who are owed close to $30million in unclaimed pension benefits. Their website features a Find an **Unclaimed Pension Tool** that can be searched by name for unclaimed pension funds. The database information about people whom PBGC has not been able to contact and does not contain information about all individuals for whom PBGC provides, or will in the future provide, a pension.

Unclaimed Pension Tool: http://search.pbgc.gov/mp/mp.aspx

The **Social Security Administration** also maintains records of individuals who qualify for certain pension benefits. When anyone applies for Social Security benefits, their name and Social Security Number are automatically checked against the pension records database and are informed if there are any matches.

Social Security Administration: http://www.ssa.gov/

The **Employee Benefits Security Administration** (EBSI) – This agency oversees retirement funds, ensuring that retirees receive the monies due to them. Their website features an **Abandoned Plan Search** tool that locates terminated retirement plans or retirement plans that are in the process of being terminated. You will need to know the name of the Retirement plan, and employer, as well as the City and State where the plan was implemented.

Employee Benefits Security Administrationo: http://www.dol.gov/ebsa/

Abandoned Plan Search: http://askebsa.dol.gov/AbandonedPlanSearch/

Federal Deposit Insurance Corporation – When a financial institution is closed by a regulatory agency, the FDIC is appointed as Receiver and is responsible for the payment of insured deposits and the liquidation of the remaining assets.

If you remember a bank account that you had forgotten about you can contact the Federal Deposit Insurance Corporation's (FDIC) Division of Resolutions and Receiverships (DRR) at 1-888-206-4662. They are able to assist consumers in tracking down the current location of accounts and recovering their funds.

You can also search a database of failed banks for accounts, including IRAs using the **FDIC Search Engine**. The search engine is ultra-sensitive to name spellings, so try several variations of your name, for instance; with and without a period after the middle initial, or with and without the middle name or middle initial, etc.

Federal Deposit Insurance Corporation:
http://www2.fdic.gov/funds/index.asp

FDIC Search Engine: http://www2.fdic.gov/funds/index.asp

Internal Revenue Service

If you believe that you are entitled to an unclaimed income tax refund, you should contact the IRS for information on how to obtain it. There are two particular types of unclaimed income tax refund:

Unfiled Income Tax Return. If you did not file a federal income tax return but believe you are due a refund, you must file a return in order to claim it. The average unclaimed refund is around $550. Federal income tax returns must be filed within three years in order for you to receive any refunds you are entitled to.
Filed an income tax return. If you filed a tax return but the check was returned to the IRS as undeliverable (perhaps you relocated and neglected to change your address with the IRS), you should visit their **Where's My Refund** web page to check the status of your refund and where you can also update your details.

Where's My Refund: http://www.irs.gov/Refunds/Where's-My-Refund-It's-Quick,-Easy,-and-Secure.

You can also telephone the IRS at 1-800-829-1954. The average amount of returned refund checks is approximately $1,150.

National Registry of Unclaimed Retirement Benefits (NRURB) - operated by PenChecks, Inc., the NRURB is the largest processor of retirement plan distributions in the United States. The registry is designed to reunite abandoned retirement plans such as pensions, 401(k)s, IRAs, and profit sharing plans with their owners.

Their database contains the names of more than 50,000 individuals who are owed retirement plan distributions, most between $500 and $1,000 in value.

National Registry of Unclaimed Retirement Benefits:
https://www.unclaimedretirementbenefits.com/

Federal Information Center

If you suspect that a Federal agency has money or property belonging to you, but need their contact number, try calling the Federal Information Center at 1-301-722-9000 or the Federal Citizen Information Center at 1-800-FED-INFO (1-800-333-4636). They can direct you to the Federal office you need to contact.

Life Insurance Company Demutualization

Many of the nation's largest life insurance companies were stated as mutual life companies, which are owned by the policyholders. When these companies became publicly traded firms through a process known as demutualization, shares of stock were issued to the policyholders in exchange for their ownership interest. When the address of the policyholder was unknown, the shares and any dividends were put into a trust fund. There are millions of policyholders, as well as their heirs, who could be entitled to these funds.

Glenn Daily, a fee-only insurance consultant, maintains a database depicting the **Reorganization Status of Mutual Life Insurance Companies** on his website. If you find your insurance company in the listing and believe you might be owed shares or money from the proceeds of the demutualization, you should contact the company directly. Be aware that if the demutualization happened more than five years ago, you will most likely be referred to the state unclaimed property office.

Reorganization Status of Mutual Life Insurance Companies:
http://www.glenndaily.com/mhctable.htm

Notes

Addresses and Phone Numbers

About the Author

Gary L. Morris has worked as a Freelance financial writer and reporter since 2009. He currently covers European Central Bank and ASEAN country developments for two large corporations and resides in Frankfurt Germany.

www.ingramcontent.com/pod-product-compliance
Lightning Source LLC
Chambersburg PA
CBHW061943280526
45787CB00004B/1713